The Unexpected

A 40-day devotional for living
with unexpected times

Iona Rossely

malcolm down

PUBLISHING

25 24 23 22   7 6 5 4 3 2 1

First published 2022 by Malcolm Down Publishing Ltd.
www.malcolmdown.co.uk
Registered Office: Welwyn Garden City, England

British Library Cataloguing in Publication Data
A catalogue record for this book is available from the British Library.

ISBN 978-1-915046-07-9

Cover painting by Iona Rossely
Cover design by Esther Kotecha
Art direction by Sarah Grace

Printed in the UK

Contents

Encouragement

Purpose

Worship

Strength

God Answered

Introduction

"Now listen, you who say, 'Today or tomorrow we will go to this or that city, spend a year there, carry on business and make money.' Why, you do not even know what will happen tomorrow. What is your life? You are a mist that appears for a little while and then vanishes. Instead, you ought to say, 'If it is the Lord's will, we will live and do this or that.'"
James 4:13-15

This is a practical guide on how to live in unexpected and changing times, knowing that whatever the world throws at you, God has you firmly under His protection. Walk with me through forty real-life experiences that will empower and strengthen your faith. I pray that you will never worry or be anxious again as our King reigns over every detail of your life. His love for you has no limits and there is nothing in this world that can separate you from His love.

Walking a supernatural life during turmoil is possible, when we trust in God. When you hand Him control of your life your journey takes on a new and exciting turn – don't miss out on what God has planned for you.

"'For I know the plans I have for you,' declares the LORD, 'plans to prosper you and not to harm you, plans to give you hope and a future.'"
Jeremiah 29:11

Trust

That's not what I'd planned

Read James 4:13-17

"Now listen, you who say, 'Today or tomorrow we will go to this or that city, spend a year there, carry on business and make money.' Why, you do not even know what will happen tomorrow."

James 4:13-14

Who in their wildest dreams would have predicted COVID-19 and the devastation it has had on the world? It was a great and mighty shock and wake-up call for many of us to realise we are not in control of our destiny. Even though I know God is sovereign and in control, when I left Dubai in March 2020 for a three-week break to our farm in Australia, I was not expecting a lockdown of over a year on the other side of the world away from my husband Jeff. We can plan all we want, but God is the only one who knows and determines our path. So here I was 11,973 kilometres away from my husband and pets, my diary was wiped clean, my travel plans cancelled, and my book launch was questionable.

Because the pandemic was on such a big scale it catapulted me out of my little micro world and launched me into looking at the world from God's perspective. God has a plan for the world and yes, a plan for each of our lives, yet we are not in a position to predict what we will do in the future, where we live, or how long we will live. We do not know God's plans, and we cannot play at being God. In a split second our lives and our world can change – and they did in March 2020.

So how do we live peacefully and serenely not knowing what will happen tomorrow? We hand tomorrow to God – we hand our plans, dreams, hopes and desires over to Him; knowing that He has our best interests at heart. Ephesians 2:10 reminds us that God has a plan set in place for each of us. "For we are his workmanship, created in Christ Jesus for good works, which God prepared beforehand, that we should walk in them." There is a great sense of freedom when you lay your plans at Jesus' feet – because you know He has your back, and He has a plan.

Prayer

Lord, forgive me when I doubt the goodness of your intentions for my life. I know you want the very best for me and that you have already mapped out a plan specifically for me. It is difficult to truly comprehend this as I do not deserve this love. I thank you from the bottom of my heart that I can live my life under your protection – I thank you that I can live knowing that where I am right now is where I should be. I am excited about my future, and I pray right now that you would instill in me a fortitude never to worry or be anxious about tomorrow. Amen

Stop, pray and let go!

Read Romans 12:9-21

"Be joyful in hope, patient in affliction, faithful in prayer."
Romans 12:12

When I jumped on a plane to Australia for a three-week break, I had no idea that Jeff and I would be apart for so long because of the pandemic. As the months drifted by it was difficult to plan a way forward. I was unable to leave Australia and Jeff was stuck in the Middle East. Every day the restrictions changed making it almost impossible to see how we could get together. We prayed for guidance and both felt strong in the fact that our faith and trust in God would keep us focused on God's will.

Jeff knuckled down and carried on working as best he could, and I was busy with the farm duties and my book launch. Jeff and I are used to being apart, but I think two months was the maximum. Now we were creeping up to the six month mark with no sign of how we could see each other. There were thousands of Australians trying to get home and only a limited number of flights; thankfully Jeff managed to get a flight back just before Christmas. He had his plane ticket and a two-week hotel quarantine booked. I was so looking forward to seeing him and also being able to celebrate Christmas together.

Leading up to his departure Jeff had a number of small gatherings at the house before he left. One of which was a couple of days before his flight with two very good friends. Little did we know that this dinner party would potentially stop Jeff from travelling home.

I rolled over in bed to turn the light off and as I did saw my phone beep a message. I was dumb struck when I read the message –

one of the dinner guests had been in contact with someone with COVID-19 so there was a possibility that Jeff would not be able to travel. This news hit me hard; we had been apart ten months and now it looked like he may not be coming home. I was numb, I was angry, and I lashed out at God – "This cannot be happening!" I screamed.

As we waited for Jeff's COVID test I still felt overwhelmed with a numb emptiness, I couldn't focus and I struggled to pray. I had a group of friends who prayed for me and I slowly felt the hand of God just resting on me and the situation. I knew God had it all in hand. I had struggled to cope when I thought Jeff wasn't coming back and I fell in the hole that the devil had set. Thankfully, through prayers and divine intervention, my perspective changed and I handed the results of the test over to God.

There is a great release when you drop your burdens and worries at the feet of Jesus. I knew whatever the result it was God's will. Jeff arrived home two weeks before Christmas.

When things don't go to plan – don't panic and rant and rave like I did – stop, pray, get your friends to pray and lay your worries at the feet of Jesus.

Prayer

Almighty God, you remind me repeatedly in the Bible not to worry or be anxious – yet sometimes I forget and lose sight of your promises. Teach me to hand over all my troubles and concerns to you in prayer. I also pray that you will stop me in my tracks before I fall into a hole of despair, yet if I do get lost in the emotions, teach me to ask for help from my praying friends. I thank you, Lord, that from this day onwards I will stop, pray, and let go of my worries. Thank you, Lord. Amen

I want an answer to my why?

Read Isaiah 55:8-11

> *"'For my thoughts are not your thoughts, neither are your ways my ways,' declares the LORD."*
> **Isaiah 55:8**

When your plans are stopped dead in their tracks, what else can you do but ask the question, "Why, God, why is this happening?" During the early stages of the pandemic I continued to ask this question day after day in my quiet time. As countries across the world started closing down their borders and travel by air no longer seemed possible, I felt a stillness descend on our farm. Our normally busy road was silent, there were no planes flying over – it was like the world was coming to a standstill. I wanted a human logical answer to my questions but instead I felt God was communicating through His silence. Sounds strange – maybe!

God reminded me of words He had placed on my heart just a year earlier – words He gave to the monk Saint Charbel, "If you do not understand my silence, you will not understand my words." I realised that in this silence I could sense God, I could hear God in the silence – that silence was God. My question was not answered in the way I expected but it was answered. The silence I felt now was one filled with power and awe and it was filled with God's glory. And in that silence came authority, sovereign control and love. This in turn led to peace – a peace that allowed me to be assured that God had the answer to the *why?*

So many times, we come to Jesus with questions and it is possible not to pick up on the answer because we are wanting the human version – we wait to hear what we want to hear, but God clearly states, "Your ways are not my ways, your thoughts are not my thoughts." So, when we ask a question and wait, we must put on our heavenly ears and listen. He hears us and answers but not always in the way we're expecting.

Prayer

Lord, I pray that I start to see the world through your eyes; so that when I'm in an uncomfortable situation my perspective is a heavenly one, not an earthly one. I know that many of my questions may not be answered but I know you hear every word I utter – show me, Lord, what I need to know in times of uncertainty and fill me with a divine peace and joy when my questions go unanswered. I thank you, Lord, for being a loving father. Amen

Focus on the invisible

Read 2 Corinthians 4:13-18

"So, we fix our eyes not on what is seen, but on what is unseen, since what is seen is temporary, but what is unseen is eternal."

2 Corinthians 4:18

I used to get angry with my dad for always having the television on – it was like he needed a connection with what was happening in the world, every second of the day. Don't get me wrong, I love to sit and watch television – normally in the evening after dinner. But at the beginning of the COVID-19 outbreak I became obsessed with having the news on all the time.

The first thing I did every morning after letting the dogs and cats out was turn on my iPad to watch the live news. At lunch time and in the evening after the horses were in bed, the news was turned on again. A couple of times I chuckled to myself thinking it must be hereditary!

As the weeks went by, I realised my news addiction was sucking me into a world of doubt, fear, and misinformation. There were so many different opinions and views – it seemed like a never-ending world of bad news. It was during my prayer time that God directed me to many Bible passages to help me refocus my mind, such as 2 Corinthians 4:18, "As we look not to the things that are seen but to the things that are unseen. For the things that are seen are transient, but the things that are unseen are eternal," was just one of many.

Why was I watching the same news over and over again? Why? I trusted God with my life – both now and when I die. So why worry? I knew there was no need to be concerned; yes, it is important to be aware of what's happening, but also to focus on what God is saying, not just humans.

The solution was easy – I started to just listen to the headlines and then turned the TV off. I love what Corrie ten Boom said on this: "If you look at the world, you'll be distressed. If you look within, you'll be depressed. But if you look at Christ, you'll be at rest." How true this is; we need to focus on Jesus only and allow Him to guide us. As we journey through life there will be patches of darkness, troubles and uncertainties but staying close to Jesus will give us a supernatural peace that surpasses all understanding.

Prayer

Lord, I pray for a more focused approach to life, one that opens my spiritual eyes to what I can't see. Lord, give me the ability to discern what is important in my life and allow me to move forward under your protection and guidance. Shift my gaze from worrying about earthly matters and teach me to keep my eyes focused on you and your will for my life. Amen

Faith

Born broken

Read Isaiah 40:25-31

> *"But those who hope in the L*ORD *will renew their strength. They will soar on wings like eagles; they will run and not grow weary, they will walk and not be faint."*

Isaiah 40:31

We live in a world where we all want perfection but in brokenness there can still be hope.

Our Arabian cross appaloosa horse Kismet was born with deformed front and back legs. Regardless of her disabilities Kismet was a fighter and determined to live life as normally as possible. As she grew, her front legs improved but her back legs got worse. She had very severe stifle locking – which meant her back knee joints would suddenly and randomly lock and she couldn't move.

The day came when Jeff and I had to choose four horses out of our twenty-three to relocate to Australia; this was a tough call. We wanted to take the three we had bred, which included Kismet, who was just two years old, plus one other. Knowing that Kismet would probably never be ridden or bred from we would have been crazy to spend that money on quarantine and flight costs. So, what did we do? We took the crazy option and Kismet was on her way to Australia!

When Kismet was five I started working her on the ground to help build muscles with the aim of maybe overcoming the joint locking and maybe getting to ride her. Sadly, when I did get on her, she panicked as her back legs locked and she was unable to move. We looked at many options, but nothing seemed to work. Did we give up on her? – no we didn't!

Three years later a light of hope appeared when our vet Greg agreed to carry out a surgical procedure that he had never done before. It was a minor operation that loosened the ligaments around the joint preventing them from "catching" or locking up. While he operated, we prayed.

A few months after the operation and months of physio I was ready to put her back into work. So, whilst in lockdown in Australia Kismet became my pet project. Slowly and gently, we worked together, every day she improved until finally I was able to ride her without any major joint lock-up issues. She now loves hacking out around the farm and playing tag in the round pen. We still have work to do, and I still believe she will improve even more. But that doesn't matter – what matters is that she's loving life and feeling useful. I look at her and I know what she's thinking, our journey over the past eight years has seen many barriers but we climbed over them together. We have a bond that cannot be broken; during the time we had together we have built a strong and powerful connection. Is Kismet a gift from God? Yes – as is every creature on this planet.

Never give up on anything that looks broken. We all come into the world broken but God never gives up on us. If we let Him, He can mould us and shape us – in this process we see hope, peace, love, and healing.

Prayer

Lord, I thank you that even though I am broken on the inside you will never give up on me and you will never leave me. Your grace and love are indescribable, I do not deserve your love; I do not deserve your protection. You, O God, are mighty in your mercy. I come in awe of your supernatural love and feel blessed to be a child – a child that is loved even in my brokenness. Lord, I pray that you will teach me to look at others who are damaged through the experiences of life to see them through your eyes – so that I can be your hands and feet and help them in their healing and lead them to your throne, where brokenness is removed. Amen

Stepping out

Read Ephesians 5:1-21

> *"Be very careful, then, how you live – not as unwise but as wise, making the most of every opportunity, because the days are evil. Therefore do not be foolish, but understand what the Lord's will is."*
>
> **Ephesians 5:15-17**

It's human reaction to retreat into a comfortable safe place when life throws curve balls and challenges at you such as the COVID-19 pandemic. It was interesting to watch how we all responded – research showed that many had stopped giving to charity and people were becoming less religious. This shocked me as I thought the opposite would happen but no, when fear sets in, we look inward and almost create a barrier around us – a bit like a tortoise retreating into their shell for safety.

God tells us repeatedly not to be afraid. He also refers to His sons and daughters on earth as an army – we are to put on the armour of God and be prepared to step out in action. Scripture tells us we are in a battle not against humans but the invisible works of the devil. We, including me, are all at fault of sometimes not stepping out in faith in situations that look and feel uncomfortable. Situations like the pandemic give us opportunities to show and highlight the power of the gospel message to those who are searching and lost.

I felt very convicted on one shopping trip to town, when I totally walked away from a God-given opportunity. A lovely older lady started chatting to me in a shopping aisle – I briefly engaged with her but was in a rush and made some feeble excuse that I needed to be somewhere. Funnily enough I ended up behind her in the cashier queue. I listened as she was telling her story to one of the other shoppers of being lonely and how she'd not been able to get home across to Queensland because of the border closures due to COVID-19. She was now camping in the agricultural grounds in town on her own – it had been twelve months and she had no idea when the lockdown would be lifted. As I listened my heart sank. I was angry with myself; I'd focused on my wants and not opened my eyes to the people God had placed in front of me.

Instead of naturally reverting to comfort we need to step out, believe and behave in ways that show the power of the living God in our lives. Where we are right now on planet earth is where God wants us to be; look around and open your eyes to the possibilities and opportunities – pray into what God wants you to do. Armies don't stand still they move forward; we need to step out in faith and allow the supernatural to move in. We can sit in front of the TV all day with food in the fridge and cupboards full of toilet rolls (important if you live in Australia!) but we are meant for so much more than that. Let God move you in the right direction and put you on the path he's planned, and let the warrior in you take hold.

Prayer

Lord, I want to do your will and step out in faith – I don't want to be a couch potato, so I pray you will instill in me the get-up-and-go fighter instinct that may have been a little dormant. Give me the strength and the courage to take bold steps into my community. Ignite in me a burning passion to spread your love and the gospel message. Turn me into a real warrior – one that hears, acts, and has a mission to do your will. Amen

Dot to dot

Read Proverbs 16:1-9

"The LORD works out everything to its proper end."
Proverbs 16:4

I find it so much easier to look at my life like a dot-to-dot drawing. As a child I would love joining the numbered dots and watch as I created a masterpiece. Now as an adult, when my plans all go skew-whiff, I know that God has already mapped out the plan of my life – a bit like a dot-to-dot drawing. I imagine myself standing on a dot and I look at the next one in terms of my future plan.

I love having goals in life – it gives me something to aim for, so when I've planned, I like to stick to it. But if you land on a dot that's not part of God's masterpiece for your life – you will end up going nowhere. You either come to a grinding halt or you go around and around in never-ending circles.

On some occasions God has placed me in a situation that was not part of my grand design and I don't hold back in telling Him, "God, I think this is wrong, this is not what we agreed." He listens to me but opens doors that move me towards the dots I'm trying to avoid. He makes the way smooth.

God has redirected me many times. I remember my journey into becoming a licensed lay minister for the Anglican church. I didn't fit the mould – especially as I struggle with religious traditions, rituals and formal church structure. I made it very clear to God that this was not on my agenda, but it turned out to be a real blessing – God placed me in a church environment that was quirky and informal, so I was able to blossom and use my skills.

It can be exciting and overwhelming but just remember He knows our gifts and strengths and will utilise them in different environments and in different seasons. So be prepared. When you invite God into leading your life – that's exactly what He will do. But it's important to have the spiritual ears to hear what He's saying so that you can follow and obey His guidance.

Be prepared, God will on occasion steer you away from your well-meaning plans to ones that are divinely guided by Him just for you. So, when you end up on a road that just doesn't fit in with your human plans, remember the masterpiece of your life is in good hands so don't fight the dot you're on – it might take you on an adventure bigger than you could have ever imagined.

Prayer

My Father in heaven, I know you watch me and you guide me every day and I thank you for this from the bottom of my heart. Give me the clarity and wisdom to know the right direction for my life. I pray, Lord, that you will reposition me if I am in the wrong place, wrong job, wrong relationship – align me with your will so that I can use the unique giftings you've given me. How amazing is your love, Lord. Amen

Faith in turmoil

Read Mark 11:22-25

"Therefore I tell you, whatever you ask for in prayer, believe that you have received it, and it will be yours."
Mark 11:24

It was heartbreaking saying goodbye to my dad who was battling stage-four cancer – we knew time was not on his side. Jeff and I had spent two weeks with my parents; in that time we prayed, laughed, and cried together. We watched Christian movies, chatted about heaven and shared in communion – these were special times.

The worry Jeff and I had was that neither my step-mum or my dad would allow anyone to help them, and both were exhausted. As we travelled back home to Dubai from America, I fervently prayed that God would guide their steps during these days. When we reached home Jeff and I prayed together and handed in faith all our worries and concerns over to our Father in heaven.

"My phone has been beeping all night with messages – what is happening?" Dozens of missed calls from an unknown American number appeared on my screen – not a good sign. I rang the number to find out it was Paul, my father's neighbour. I listened in shock as he told me that Kathleen had collapsed and had been taken to hospital which left my dad alone and with no support. Paul offered to help, along with his wife. My immediate reaction was to jump on a plane and go back but a small voice inside of me said, "Have faith – you handed this situation to God, and He is dealing with it."

It is so hard when you're thousands of miles away and you can't help; all we could do was pray. I couldn't understand what God was doing – why had this not happened a week earlier when we were there? We could have helped, why wait until we had landed back home? – it didn't make sense.

Weeks later it did – God had a plan. While I only saw the negative, God had created a situation that would bring in help for both my parents. Kathleen had collapsed out of exhaustion from taking care of my dad twenty-four hours of the day, she agreed to six weeks of rest whilst my dad, who had refused outside help, was now getting nurse care, physio care and his church family were all actively involved helping both. Kathleen also became involved in a new Bible study group and ended up with many new Christian friends. Through this curve ball God created a support group around them, and in this turmoil He built a path that would lead my parents closer to Him.

Have faith and trust when you cry out for help – God acts to help not to destroy. He hears and answers.

Prayer

Almighty God, instill in me a deeper steadfast faith that allows me never to doubt or waver from what I believe. Give me the resilience of a warrior to know that you hear my prayers and will answer in your divine timing. Help me to understand that your answers to my prayers maybe different from what I expect – and that everything you do in my life will only strengthen and guide me in my walk with you. Amen

God in the details

Read Matthew 10:29-33

"Are not two sparrows sold for a penny? Yet not one of them will fall to the ground outside your Father's care."

Matthew 10:29

Our pets have always been a big part of our life. Jeff and I couldn't have children, so I suppose our menagerie of dogs, cats and horses are our family. The loss of just one of these faithful companions is heartbreaking; no matter how much you prepare yourself, each time I feel like my heart is ripped out and crushed with sorrow. I may be slightly overly passionate about my pets, but I know, like us, their life span is limited. I've learnt that every day with them is a blessing.

I couldn't imagine living on the farm without my guard dog and companion Shiraz, but it looked like she was coming to the end of her time – the thought alone brought tears to my eyes. Her breathing was laboured, and she was struggling to keep up on the walks with the other dogs; x-rays showed two large black shadows on her lungs. Operating was not an option as she was nearing her time, the only thing we could do was pray. Then the unexpected happened; our six-year-old Rottweiler Samson and Shiraz's best mate got sick – so sick he had to be put down,

"This can't be happening!" I screamed, but it did. Having lost one dog and knowing that Shiraz didn't have long totally threw me. Shiraz was also heartbroken and she rapidly started fading in front of my eyes, I just felt numb.

But in that numbness God put a thought in my head, "Red Doberman puppy." I wrote it down in my journal. Why would I want a Doberman? It's the only dog that had ever bitten me!

I researched their characteristics and found they were loyal, intelligent and great guard dogs, but unfortunately there were none available in the whole of Australia. But God had one in mind! Amanda, who worked for us, was always up for a challenge and within a couple of weeks of searching the internet she found one red Doberman puppy. Two months later our new addition, George, was on the farm. It wasn't long before Shiraz and George were playing, Shiraz's health started to improve, and her medication was halved. I was still asking myself was this the right move getting another puppy when God put on my heart to check George's date of birth. To my utter surprise he was born exactly two days after Samson passed – this was not a coincidence.

I believe that God chooses the pets he's going to put in your care. God is a God of details – there is nothing that you do, think, or say that he doesn't want to be involved in. Allow God into every aspect of your life, He wants to be actively involved. So be open to thoughts that pop into your head. If they come out of the blue, don't dismiss them; thoughts are one way that God interacts with us. And as I write this devotional one year on, Shiraz is still with us, an absolute miracle. Every day we have with her we count as a blessing.

Prayer

Almighty God, I am so blessed to know that you are in all the details of my life – how amazing that you care and love me so much that you want to be involved in all my decision making. Don't let me forget this today or any other day, I need to learn to pray into everything not just the big things in life. I stand before you today wanting you to be in, around and involved in every aspect of my life. Amen

Frustrated

Read Jeremiah 29:10-14

> *"'For I know the plans I have for you,' declares the LORD, 'plans to prosper you and not to harm you, plans to give you hope and a future.'"*
> **Jeremiah 29:11**

There are seasons in your life when everything you do seems to fall down a bottomless pit and you feel hollow and empty on the inside. The devil is very cunning when you're in what many call a dry season – your prayers don't seem to be answered, you lack direction, and you just feel like you're bobbing along without any support. Even though God is busy working behind the scenes to make straight your path, the devil takes full advantage by planting doubts in your mind about everything.

I recently had such a season. Day by day I was becoming more frustrated, things were just not happening; prayers seemed to pop into outer space and never reach God, His presence also seemed to have vanished. *Why do I feel like this? Why do I feel frustrated all the time? Why do I feel like I'm like a dog chasing its tail – around and around in circles – going nowhere!*

In one of many conversations with God I was whining about my frustrations and that I was in desperate need of some guidance. Anyway, He did answer me, but it wasn't what I'd expected,

"Iona, stop trying to play God, stop trying to control everything. Let it go and just give everything to me." He was right. I'd fallen back into trying to control everything and was becoming more and more frustrated when things weren't going my way. God had a plan and I needed to let Him do His will and not interfere. The word faith means trust – I needed to trust in God's goodness for my life – even when I didn't understand the season I was in.

Don't make the mistake of taking back control as this only moves you off the path He has ordained for you, "'For I know the plans I have for you,' declares the LORD" (Jeremiah 29:11). I've learnt that it's ok to wait. We live in a push button society that is not good at waiting. Be patient and pray into your situation and ask the Lord to put peace in your heart. That peace will allow you to make the most of the time. Sometimes God will ask you to put your life on pause whilst he reshuffles things, situations, people, etc., to set the path straight for your journey. Enjoy the waiting season knowing that God is in this and on this – remember He has a plan to give you hope and a future.

Prayer

Lord, how exciting that you know the plan for my life – and, Lord, I pray from today onwards that I will never doubt you or fall into the trap of despair when life looks bleak. Give me the inner strength to stay strong and positive in every situation. I thank you for the promises, especially the one to give me hope and a future. Amen

JOY

SELF CONTROL

IENCE

FAITHFULNESS

GENTLENESS

PEACE

GOODNESS

KINDNESS

LOVE

Christian Living

It's still a mystery

Read Acts 5:12-16

"As a result, people brought the sick into the streets and laid them on beds and mats so that at least Peter's shadow might fall on some of them as he passed by."

Acts 5:15

"Would you like to visit a monastery – its famous because the tomb of Saint Charbel is in there?" I looked at Jeff and then back to our Lebanese friend Imad, "Not sure! But if you think it's worth the visit then why not," I said. I wasn't jumping up and down with excitement but since our five-day trip to Beirut had been non-stop rain, tourist options were limited.

Imad cheerfully uploaded all the information on the Maronite monk as we drove up the steep mountain. Most of what he said I dismissed as being a bit far-fetched. Yes, I have seen miracles and witnessed supernatural healings, but I did struggle with a deceased monk in a tomb being able to heal today. How wrong could I be.

The monastery was buzzing with people. As we strolled around the historic building, I did feel like I had been transported back in time. As we came to the end of the visit, we entered the last room that housed the tomb of St Charbel, it was behind a wrought iron gate that reached to the ceiling. The story goes that his body never decomposed, it just kept oozing bodily fluids and because of this they would rewrap his body and rehouse him in a different coffin.

Jeff, Imad and David, another friend, all ignored the tomb and went off looking at icons along the grey stone walls. I felt drawn towards the tomb and as I peered through the open iron bars

I suddenly felt overcome with a presence that had me drop to my knees. I had no idea what was happening – I just felt a warm, peaceful, glowing presence all around me. I did not want to move, instead I knelt next to two elderly gentlemen who were deep in prayers whilst I bathed in what I knew was God's glory.

I didn't want to leave the tomb, but Imad, Jeff and David were all waiting at the exit for me; I was still trying to process my experience as I ignored all the strange looks from Jeff and company and left the site. This whole experience threw me a little because I couldn't explain what had happened, I just knew that this was a place where God healed, and a place where heaven and earth connected. Sometimes we must accept the mysteries that God allows us to experience – even if we don't understand them. For me this was a lesson on being open to different godly experiences that defy human logic.

Prayer

Lord, you are a God of wonder, and your mercies are unending. I know that spending time in your presence permeates light into my very being, and that same divine light can be seen and felt by believers and non-believers. Like the apostle Peter and Saint Charbel, they were devoted men who lived and breathed only you. I know that there is nothing more important than spending time in your presence so that I can immerse myself in who you are and clothe my very being with your glory. How awesome is your power, O mighty God. Amen

I died again and again

Read 2 Corinthians 5:16-21

"Therefore, if anyone is in Christ, the new creation has come: the old has gone, the new is here!"
2 Corinthians 5:17

There is a saying in the sporting world that states "An athlete dies twice", once when he retires and again at the end of life. When I fell at 160kph in a speed skiing race I was blessed not to die, yet on the inside I did. My identity was stripped away, I felt like I had lost part of who I was. My world up until the near-fatal crash had been totally dedicated to skiing. My shattered right leg was now metal and with twelve months of rehabilitation my sporting career was in ruins. Emotionally I was weak and exhausted . . . who was I? I had no idea!

Several years on I was back competing, against the orders of the doctors, this time racing endurance on the Irish Equestrian Team. I was doing what I do best – competing. For eight years I competed in all the major international events as one of the top-six Irish riders. That was until a major incident that meant for the first time I hadn't qualified for the World Equestrian Games. My world literally fell apart, I was unable to process this failure and I went into meltdown. In my book *Racing on Empty*, I wrote, "It was like something inside of me had died." The sense of loss and feeling of emptiness was indescribable. I look back and say yes, I died twice – but there was a third imminent death approaching.

I was in a dark emotional place – one that felt like a bottomless pit with no way out. But it was in my despair that I came face to face with God. Whilst standing in His presence I suddenly realised I had it all wrong – I needed to let go of controlling my destiny and hand my life over to the one who loved me more than anyone else.

In that moment I experienced sudden peace and freedom, all the pressure, burdens and deadlines I had created myself were removed. I cried tears of joy – I felt a freedom I had never experienced before – it was a freedom that allowed me to be me. I knew then that my identity was not based on what I achieved or what I did. I was unique and loved by my Creator and He had a plan for my life; one that would give me everlasting life and no more emotional deaths. I suppose I thought that by letting go of the controls of my life, God would step in and change my personality and take away all the things I loved. How wrong could I be. God gave us our personality and our passions, now I could utilise my gifts under His direction and for His glory.

In surrendering my life to God, I felt like the old me had died and a new me was born. In a twinkling of an eye my world had turned upside down. I was a new person. The apostle Paul said, "I die daily" (1 Corinthians 15:31 KJV) showing all of us that to follow Christ we need to surrender over our lives on a daily basis. By emptying ourselves we allow God to connect, guide and use us in a powerful way.

Prayer

Lord, there is nothing more important than to walk the road you have planned for me. I pray that from today I will surrender over all the controls of my life to you each morning. Give me the strength and the courage to let go of the worries, burdens, habits and anything else that stops me from walking with you. I am happy to die to myself each day and live a life focused on you and you alone. I thank you, Lord, my King, my God. Amen

Divine protection is for real!

Read Psalm 91:1-16

"For he will command his angels concerning you to guard you in all your ways; they will lift you up in their hands, so that you will not strike your foot against a stone. You will tread upon the lion and the cobra; you will trample the great lion and the serpent."

Psalm 91:11-13

There are so many promises in the Bible relating to how God protects us; however, we can read over them and not really take on board their relevance for our lives. That is until we come face to face with danger. I had been reading Psalm 91 almost daily – the words are comforting and give us reassurance; but this one week, shortly after the World Health Organization announced that COVID-19 was officially a pandemic, God reminded me that Psalm 91 was for real.

One Monday afternoon as I was rushing from the stables to the house, I stood on an Eastern brown snake, one of the deadliest snakes in Australia. I screamed and leapt into the air! Thankfully the snake was as shocked as I was and shot off into the bushes. My heart skipped a beat. I chose to forget about the encounter until the following Monday when, as I was walking through our garden, I stood on yet another Eastern brown – even larger than the last one. This time it reared up and launched itself at my leg. What! My sunglasses flew off my head and actually landed on the snake – which distracted him for a split second – so I ran, managing to get away from the danger.

The fact that I had this encounter with two different deadly snakes, in two different locations but on the same day a week apart, led me to believe this was no coincidence but a message. God reminded me of the verse in Psalm 91: "You will tread upon the lion and the cobra; you will trample the great lion and the serpent. 'Because he loves me,' says the LORD, 'I will rescue him; I will protect him, for he acknowledges my name.'"

The day you become a follower of Jesus and submit control of your life to Him a divine connection is made. And with that connection comes all the promises of the Bible including how He watches over us and protects us. This does not mean that we'll never be sick or get injured; what it means is that He is watching out for us, in every step we take, in every situation we're in. God's protection is like a large umbrella – when we walk with Him, we are covered. And if sickness or injury happen whilst we're under that umbrella we can rest in the knowledge that God is protecting us – no matter what.

Prayer

Lord, how awesome to know that I am never alone – that you are always by my side. How amazing is it that you watch over every step I take. I thank you that I have no need to fear as you are my refuge, my rock and my great protector. Amen

Stay connected

Read James 4:7-10

"Come near to God and he will come near to you."
James 4:8

The first couple of weeks of being in lockdown on the farm felt like everything was in slow motion. Even though we were busy with the horses and cattle I had a dedicated quiet time with God and His presence seemed to stay with me during the day. But with my book launch just around the corner my schedule started filling up with radio and TV interviews, photo shoots and discussions around marketing and public relations plans to help the book. I felt like I was on a roller-coaster. My quiet time was getting shorter as my focus had shifted away from God to my own priorities. I had lost that awareness of God's presence, even though I knew /He was with me – I felt disconnected.

I function better when I have a set time for prayer and study, gym workout, riding and walking the dogs; that way I can be semi organised. We are all creatures of habit, so it does work; but we still need to prioritise. God has given us the freedom to choose how we spend our days so it's up to us – the ball is in our court. I started to wonder where the time went each day; I was up early walking the dogs, had a quick prayer and Bible study time, ate breakfast, and then rode one of the horses before the heat set in. The rest of the day was packed with book-launch events and farm administration. Each day I promised myself that I would spend more time with Jesus but as soon as the world woke up, I got sucked into it – I was busy, very busy, but also very disconnected.

After a couple of months my longing for more of Jesus thankfully catapulted me into a totally different mindset. I rewrote my schedule. I was now getting up at five a.m., praying, studying God's words and sitting in silence at His feet. My world changed – my outlook changed. I now felt connected to God. I was no longer on a roller-coaster; I had peace even in the busyness of the day and I saw God actively working in my life.

Starting your day with Jesus allows you to stay connected – it's a bit like plugging in a power socket and switching it on – remember we can do nothing without been connected to God (John 15:4-5). And yes, I have a power nap in the afternoon!

Prayer

Lord, I pray for a more disciplined life; one that allows me to stay connected to you throughout the whole day. Help me reshuffle my daily schedule so that I can start my day with you. You know all the ins and outs of my daily routine so I hand my busy schedule over to you right now, knowing that you will guide me and give me the inward strength to be more disciplined. I thank you, Lord, that I can walk with you and be with you every second and minute of my day. Amen

Remove the box

Read Isaiah 55:1-13

"As the heavens are higher than the earth, so are my ways higher than your ways and my thoughts than your thoughts."

Isaiah 55:9

It is normal for many of us to love structure as we are able to navigate through life knowing we have some sort of plan. But the structure that makes us feel more comfortable can also stop us from experiencing the blessings of God in our lives. I see structure as a box – as we put all our prayed plans and goals in this box, we unknowingly limit ourselves. When we live in the light of all God's promises we don't need that box.

Some structure is good when it is flexible and versatile. My quiet time was always the same – repent, pray and read the Bible. Then I added singing worship songs to the mix along with periods of total silence where I just sat in the presence of God. Every day it changes as I now allow the prompting of the Holy Spirit to guide me. Life lived outside of a box is so much more exciting!

We also tend to put God in a box – God has no limits to what He can do in our lives – He doesn't have a box to confine Him. We need to think outside of the box and our greatest help in revamping how we think is the supernatural power we have inside of us – the Holy Spirit.

Jesus said, "But I tell you the truth: it is to your good that I am going away, the Counsellor will not come to you; but if I go, I will send him to you" (John 16:7).

Don't limit yourself or limit God by putting up walls of structure – allow the Holy Spirit the freedom to create opportunities in your daily life. Be receptive to His guidance and allow Him to open doors into new and exciting days. As Jesus said, the Holy Spirit is here to help us journey through life – so connect with Him and allow Him to move you out of your comfort zone – the box you have created – which in turn will bring blessings for you and glory to God.

Prayer

Lord God Almighty, how I stand in awe of your power and majesty. I know sometimes I forget that you can turn my life around in a split second – help me to pray big prayers knowing that there is nothing you cannot do. I pray that the Holy Spirit would step in right now and guide me into a life that has no walls or boundaries. I don't want to live in a box that holds me back; teach me to live a life where everything is possible and the gifts you have given me are utilised for your glory. Amen

Godly dreams

Read Joel 2:28-32

"And afterwards, I will pour out my Spirit on all people. Your sons and daughters will prophesy, your old men will dream dreams, your young men will see visions."
Joel 2:28

I've had several God dreams which I know came from God; when you have them there are no doubts, you just know you know it came from heavenly realms.

"Jeff, Jeff, wake up – you won't believe this!" He rolled over and grunted, "It's two in the morning, Iona, I don't want to know." He rolled over and went back to sleep.

I lay there processing over and over the dream that I had just had . . . I had been standing in our lounge talking to several friends who were standing in front of a large glass window that reached way up to the roofline. As I was talking, I saw a huddle of angels descending and ascending behind the glass.

I was so mesmerised by them that I slowly walked towards them, then the glass seemed to disappear. The angels kept moving up and down, then one of the angels brushed my arm; suddenly I was overwhelmed by an emotion I'd never felt before and would struggle to describe. It was like peace, joy and bliss all rolled into one; it was so powerful that I felt myself pass out.

The next morning while walking the dogs and having breakfast I kept rambling on and on to Jeff in detail about the vivid dream that I had experienced. He remained silent, no comments, no wise remarks, he just decided to remain in mute mode.

I recorded my experience in my journal and also drew what I had seen. Confirmation came that my encounter was very real at our prayer, praise and pizza evening which we hosted every Wednesday. There were ten of us praying in our living room when Joe suddenly said, "I see this house surrounded by angels and they are descending and ascending." Jeff nearly fell over backwards – he looked over at me with a "that's amazing!" expression.

My heart leapt – thank you, Lord! I went on to tell everyone in the room about my dream and showed them my journal and the pictures I'd drawn. It was as though God wanted to reaffirm that the angels were here and in this place. That evening the Holy Spirit touched each of us in an extraordinary way.

Don't dismiss your dreams and stay alert to how God confirms that those dream encounters are real.

Prayer

My Father in heaven, how awesome is it that you want to have a relationship with me. I thank you that there are so many ways that you communicate with me – from dreams, visions, thoughts, people, creation and through your word. Lord, give me a heightened awareness to hear and see when you speak into my life. Please don't let me miss out on connecting with you – help me to stay alert and watchful today and every day. Amen

Prayer

Miracle cows

Read Matthew 19:26-30

"Jesus looked at them and said, 'With man this is impossible, but with God all things are possible.'"
Matthew 19:26

We live on a farm with cattle and horses in the most stunning countryside of Northern New South Wales and are blessed with awesome neighbours. Sadly, we were brokenhearted to hear one of our neighbours Phil had been given only a couple of months to live. Shortly after hearing this news Phil called to ask if we would take his four pet cows. I did not hesitate to say yes but within seconds of putting my mobile down I was overcome with dread. What had I committed to?

These weren't four sweet, cuddly, cute cows, they were more bordering on the wild, feral variety. They had no respect for fencing, barbed wire or electric and had acquired amazing skills in jumping or barging through boundaries. I had met Merlin the leader of the herd on a couple of occasions as I drove (maybe too fast) around a corner – there he was standing in the middle of the road – he knew he was a 1000-kilo steer with very long horns and used this to his advantage.

We took a week to try and befriend Merlin and co. before we moved them. This meant keeping them in a small cattle yard overnight with lots of delicious food. Each morning we returned to find no cows – they'd jumped out. This is not normal cow behaviour!

After reinforcing the cattle yard, the time had now come to walk them from our neighbours' property to the other side of our farm, across nine paddocks, through eight gates, past our ten horses and thirty cattle into our cattle yard. Everyone said we were mad – it was dangerous and foolish for us and our livestock. Realistically there was nothing stopping these four renegades from demolishing all our fencing and injuring our livestock. Had we taken on too much? I had been praying about this and felt God say we needed to get together and pray. So, the morning of the cow move, myself, and the three girls who worked for us knelt down on the grass next to our four bemused cows and prayed – we prayed hard – we knew this was impossible without God's help and protection.

Amanda and Tegan led the way as the four very calmy followed; Melinda and I stayed at the rear. We watched in amazement as they strolled happily along – at one point it was like they were in a tunnel with yellow light surrounding them. Plus, there was this sense of peace in the air – the whole thing was beyond supernatural. It took us forty minutes to walk them one kilometre. We thought it would take us one day. When we got them into our cattle yard, we all collapsed on our knees thanking God. For me one of the greatest lessons here was the power of prayer within a group – as you kneel, pray and hold hands just watch what God can do. Never, ever underestimate the power of prayer.

Prayer

Lord, every word I speak and think you hear. There is not one word you do not hear – Lord, teach me to be more of a prayer warrior in my daily life. Help me to constantly stay in communication with you, as the apostle Paul taught us, we must pray without ceasing. And when challenges are set in front of me, I know that when we gather in your name miracles can happen. Lord, I want a supernatural life and one that glorifies your name. How awesome are you, my Lord – how awesome is your name. Amen

Crying from the heart

Read Jeremiah 29:4-14

"Then you will call on me and come and pray to me, and I will listen to you."

Jeremiah 29:12

When my pets, that are so precious to me, pass on, I feel like a little bit of my heart goes with them. No matter how much I prepare, the sadness tears me apart. But the very worst is when one goes missing and you have no idea if they are lying hurt or trapped somewhere – the not knowing sends me into an emotional dive.

Jesus knows our heart and thus knows our passions. So, when we lost Chloe, one of our Arabian rescued cats, I prayed desperately for her safe return. We had only recently flown in four dogs and four cats from Dubai to Australia – all of which were rescued bar one, Lady Bella the Italian Greyhound. Our cats are all trained to come in at night and are used to roads and traffic, so we were rather bemused by Chloe's disappearance. But then we also needed to take into account that the Australian wildlife such as snakes and foxes may have had something to do with her absence.

A week passed and still no sign. Now I knew to expect the worst. It was the not knowing bit that pulled at my heart strings. As I drove home from the shops I screamed out to God *"Please, Lord, I just need closure – what happened to her? Just let me know what happened to her."* I prayed for the whole journey home. On returning to the farm, I found myself unable to open our front gate – some bright spark had lifted the gate up and wrapped the chain so tight I was unable to release the catch. I needed someone to help.

I called Amanda who was on her lunch break – she opted to cycle along the main road instead of coming across the paddocks as she normally did. When she turned up, she looked visibly upset.

"I could smell something bad, so I pulled up and went searching – I found Chloe." Both of us burst into tears. Chloe had been knocked by a car and thrown into the bushes. It wasn't what I wanted to hear but it was an answer to the prayer I had prayed earlier when I asked God to let me know what had happened to her.

You may see this as a rather morbid subject, but bad things do happen – I personally believe every pet goes to heaven so the sadness is softened. This whole experience showed me that God heard my cry of pain and answered. It was answered by the electrician incorrectly closing the gate followed by Amanda's unexpected cycle ride along the main road. God answers the cries from our hearts, we just need to ask.

Prayer

Almighty God, how blessed am I that you hear every word I speak in prayer. I thank you, Lord, that when life throws curve balls at me, you comfort me and fill me with heavenly peace. Help me to pray into all situations so that I can open the gateway into heavenly realms and see your glory descend bringing your divine light into darkness. I love you, Lord. Amen

Flying fur

Read 1 John 5:13-21

"And if we know that he hears us – whatever we ask – we know that we have what we asked of him."
1 John 5:15

Samson, an eight-week-old puppy, hung onto my leg with a vice-like grip and he wasn't letting go!

"No, don't buy him, he's the runt of the litter," said the breeder. How could I choose, they were all so cute – there must have been twenty Rottweiler puppies running and playing, except for Samson who was still attached to my leg. It was a no-brainer – Samson was the one. We knew he had joint issues, so when the vet gave him two to three years of quality life, we accepted it and moved on. Samson was goofy, fun loving, obsessed with balls and a great companion for our other big dog Shiraz. Years went by with no major health issues. He was the prefect dog in every way except he hated cats, I mean really hated cats!

Life became a little more complicated when we relocated our pets from Dubai to our farm in Australia, which included four cats, but now we had to come up with a plan on how to teach Samson to love cats. I prayed for months that God would intervene. We also used some human wisdom – or lack of it, by coming up with a unique training plan that would help. We attached a big fluffy cat toy to a remote-control car which could travel up to 40kph. As Samson's weakness was chasing cats I would teach him not to chase the remote fluffy feline – what could go wrong?! Samson took one look at this high-speed fur ball and ran in the opposite direction – into the house! We couldn't stop laughing. Best to leave this in God's hands, I thought.

Two weeks before our cats were due to arrive Samson suddenly started to show severe signs of joint malfunction. After several trips to the vets, it was clear we may lose him. When he was unable to use his back legs, he was put to sleep. My heart broke in two, the pain was crippling but I just knew in my heart the time was right. Samson had lived three years longer than expected and now, just a week before our cats arrived, he had been called home to Jesus.

Sometimes our prayers are answered in ways that don't make sense. I look back and see we were able to give Samson six happy years on the farm, longer than predicted, and now our four rescued cats could have a stress-free life on our farm.

God knows even when a sparrow falls from a branch in your garden, He is aware of every detail of your life. He is a good father who paves the way for the future – sometimes it means sad days may be ahead but rest assured, He is in control.

Prayer

I thank you, Lord, that you are with me through all my ups and downs on planet earth. I know that testing times will happen, and that seasons of sadness and happiness will come and go, but I know that throughout my journey you are holding my hand and guiding me towards eternal life. Lord, let me not get dragged down into dark emotions when things go wrong but to have a quiet assurance of joy – because you are my rock and refuge. Amen

Encouragement

Jesus sets the stage

Read Deuteronomy 31:1-8

"The LORD himself goes before you and will be with you; he will never leave you nor forsake you. Do not be afraid; do not be discouraged."

Deuteronomy 31:8

No one on this planet would have imagined that the whole world would be struck down by a deadly pandemic – but we were. Why? That's only an answer God can give us. But I know that He positioned all His children in the right location surrounded by the right people, knowing that this was about to happen. What do I mean by this? The Lord goes ahead of each of His followers and plans – he sets the stage.

A couple of months prior to COVID-19 I was in Dubai and got a call from our farm manager to say she was resigning after three years. I had an inkling this may happen as they had just purchased their own property, also she was pregnant. The issue was finding someone to replace her. From previous experience I knew this wasn't easy; finding reliable, trustworthy staff had proved difficult. I had just arrived back in Dubai from Australia so returning was out of the question. So here I was, 11,900 plus kilometres from the farm, wondering how on earth could I find the right person for the job.

I sat down to pray into this and immediately felt God say the problem was already solved. I had no idea what that meant but I had a real sense of peace; normally I would be in panic mode, especially when it comes to the welfare of the dogs, horses and cattle. The days went by, and I kept getting the same message, "It's simple – it's all sorted." It sounds crazy but that's what I heard.

I still knew I had to step out and start looking so I messaged a couple of horsey friends to see if they knew of anyone. As I was messaging, I saw a Facebook friend who hadn't posted online for a while. Amanda had previously worked for us part time and had moved on to a full-time job. On the off chance I sent her a message about the up-and-coming job with the hope she could recommend someone. Within a minute she came back and said she was interested. Wow! She was the perfect person for the job.

Later I found out that as she had been lying on her bed and praying for help, she was feeling low and despondent, desperate for a change; my message popped up on her phone. A year down the track and I still cannot believe what a blessing Amanda has been. She stepped in to manage 270 acres, 60 cattle and ten horses. God always places the right people with you when you have to battle through certain situations such as COVID-19 and the lockdown restrictions. I would have been on my own if God hadn't sent her and, vice versa, Amanda loves her role here and has grown in her faith; she has become a crucial player in keeping the farm running and has also become a good friend. God knew both of us would be away from family and friends – so He orchestrated a plan that would see us thrive not suffer.

Don't panic when you face a situation that seems unsolvable, instead pray and then listen – God knows what is around the corner and has set the stage ready for your next adventure.

Prayer

Lord, how exciting and reassuring to know that you go before me and set the stage for my journey here on earth. Thank you, Lord, that you watch over me and keep me on the road that is uniquely mine. I pray that I don't drift off course but come to you in prayer about everything, and when challenges come my way remind me that you knew this was going to happen and you are with me. I thank you, Lord, that through the ups and downs of life I can stand firm knowing you have sorted out my future and more. Amen

Unexpected news

Read Ecclesiastes 3:1-14

"There is a time for everything, and a season for every activity under the heavens."

Ecclesiastes 3:1

Three to four months into the world pandemic I received an email from a lady stating she was Jeff's cousin. She was asking for information regarding surnames to confirm that they were related, and if they were, she had news regarding Jeff's father, Harold. Not really thinking too much about this I forwarded the message to Jeff.

Jeff's father had walked out on him when he was only three and it had left a very deep emotional scar – even sixty-five years on Jeff carried this hurt deep down and never really wanted to talk about it; it was like a piece of his heart had hardened to the point that even God couldn't get in. Being abandoned by a parent cuts deep into your very being – you feel like those scars will never heal. But with God's help and in His timing they can.

The emails started flying backwards and forwards; Jeff now had acquired loads of new cousins he'd never met. Out of this connection came news of his father – news that turned Jeff's life upside down.

Jeff knew very little about his dad except that he had been a prisoner of war and as a result of this he had come back traumatised and used alcohol to help him cope. Alcohol destroyed the marriage and Harold walked out leaving Jeff and his mum Judy. That was the last any one had heard of him. Jeff didn't know if his dad was alive or dead – thankfully the cousins were able to fill in all the gaps and more. Harold had spent a great deal of time in a concentration camp and had on many occasions put his life at risk to help save friends. Post-traumatic stress hit him hard on returning home and he became an alcoholic. The cousins met him and knew him well – he was known as the black sheep of the family but something extraordinary happened in his later years. Whilst in jail in Kalgoorlie, Harold gave his life to Jesus. The cousins said it was a radical conversion – he totally changed. He gave up the alcohol overnight and spent most of his time evangelising and spreading the good news of the gospel wherever he went.

Hearing about his dad's conversion totally overwhelmed Jeff – knowing that his father had been saved meant that he was now able to allow the walls around his heart to fall. Since a child Jeff had hidden behind this protective barrier, now that wall was crumbling. Along with the good news of Harold becoming a Christian there was the sad news that his dad had passed away. But Jeff now knew he would see his earthly dad again – in heaven. I know Jeff's heart was crying for joy inside – mine was!

There are times in our lives when our hearts are broken, and our emotional scars look like they'll never heal – but Jesus knows – He knows when to step in and heal.

Prayer

Lord, I know you have a perfect timing for everything that happens in my life. I feel so blessed knowing that you have set out certain seasons that will mould and strengthen me in my walk with you. Teach me to be more prayerful and patient in my daily life and not to get concerned when I don't get an immediate response to my prayers. I pray that as I wait on you, Lord, I will begin to understand the true meaning of your divine and glorious timing for my life. Amen

Act on opportunities

Read Ephesians 5:8-20

> *"Making the most of every opportunity, because the days are evil."*
>
> **Ephesians 5:16**

Sometimes God will stop you dead in your tracks – which is what happened for most of us during the pandemic. Many would have asked the question, "what now?" I did! And I got an answer almost immediately.

For many years I've had in my heart to start a worship service at the farm but never had time to do it, partly because of my travel schedule. Now I had the opportunity, even in the midst of the pandemic, to worship under the heavens surrounded by God's glorious creation – no buildings, no manmade structures – just open. I also had the chance to create a worship environment that would appeal to so many in our community. I knew there were people who are often uncomfortable about walking into church buildings so this was a chance not to be missed.

A year on and our outdoor worship service has blossomed under God's guidance. We are called PPP which stands for Prayer, Praise and Pecan – as we gather under a very large pecan tree. We have people from all denominations and many non-believers who are on a journey – it's relaxed, it's a safe space, one built on God's love. The best bit is worshipping (singing) and having all God's creation join in. We've had birds singing and circling us – we've had two eagles appear plus the horses seem to revel in the atmosphere – the dogs that come stay quiet and normally end up lying on their backs with four paws in the air. The ambiance is one of serenity, peace and a divine stillness.

At the beginning of PPP our beautiful neighbour came over just to join us for coffee after the worship; she arrived as we were singing our last song. She said she was transfixed as it was all so supernatural – when we sang, hundreds of birds circled the pecan tree; she had no idea what was happening she just knew she needed to be part of the group – since that day she has never missed a worship service.

We worship in many forms but to be outside singing alongside all of God's creation is the best. So, when things don't go as planned – remember God can create the opportunities He's placed on our hearts in times when we are not expecting them.

Prayer

Almighty God, I thank you that even in what seems like dark and gloomy times you give us pathways to light – your divine light. I pray, Lord, that I do not miss out on opportunities that you place in front of me. Open my spiritual eyes today so I can look outside of my situation and see with new eyes what you have planned. Place in my heart the passion for what needs to be done and give me the wisdom to see and act accordingly. Amen

You only need Jesus

Read Proverbs 16:1-10

"In their hearts humans plan their course, but the LORD establishes their steps."

Proverbs 16:9

Sometimes we can plan and plan – but if God wants a different path for us, it is always for the better.

After nine months in lockdown, we were able to open up our small country church. There was great excitement and lots of preparation in putting together this service, from the music, to the sermon preparation to getting the liturgy onto the PowerPoint for the big screen; in addition we had the COVID-19 restrictions to follow and put in place. Due to the diversity of our community, we have a traditional service on one Sunday and then a more informal charismatic worship service on the other. Today was the more traditional version led by the minister Lyndon.

Things started to go wrong fairly early on when the computer decided not to connect to the big screen. We did everything possible: we changed the cables, turned everything off and on, rebooted the system and even laid hands on the computer asking for divine intervention – nothing! This had never happened before. We came to the decision that we had a faulty cable, and we'd have to read from the printed Sunday pamphlet instead.

"Lyndon, where is the box with the pamphlets?" I shouted as he walked into the church. Having rushed from one church service to this one, along with his wife Anna and their two boys – I knew by the expression on his face that the box never made it. At this point I thought Lyndon was going into meltdown – we had nothing. We prayed for divine intervention and we got it. Anna sang and played the keyboard beautifully whilst Lyndon did everything ad lib. Lyndon likes everything set out in black and white, so this was not a natural environment for him – but when Jesus takes centre stage everything falls into place.

The words spoken and sung were Spirit filled to the point that there was an overwhelming sense of God's presence. God had taken control. It was a lesson to all of us that we don't always need pre-planned words or an entertainment schedule, we just need Jesus at the centre and core of what we do, the Holy Spirit will do the rest.

In whatever you do, if Jesus is at the core of it, then your steps will be divinely guided.

Prayer

Lord, teach me not to fret when my plan or schedule for the day doesn't go to plan. Help me to understand that you are a God that wants to be involved in every detail of my life. Allow me today to see your hand at work even in the unplanned events and situations. I thank you that you reign over every situation in my life. Thank you, Lord. Amen

Storms of life

Read Matthew 11:25-30

"Come to me, all you who are weary and burdened, and I will give you rest."

Matthew 11:28

I was preparing a talk on how to live with a supernatural peace even when life bombards you with negative troublesome stuff. Little did I know that God was going to test the well-known phrase "practice what you preach" whilst I put my message together. I've experienced many storms in life and know that if I surrender the controls of my life first thing every morning – I know that God has my back through the good stuff and the bad.

Running a 270-acre farm and looking after six dogs, two brave cats and eight horses was the norm – so occasionally it gets hectic but the week leading up to my sermon went to the extreme in craziness! It started with our dog Bentley ripping out his dew claw on our morning walk, which also turned into the poor dog having seven teeth out, which meant multiple trips to the vets.

Next I had to throw out all the food from our freezer as it suddenly stopped working. Later we found a mouse had eaten through the computer board in the back of the freezer – a mouse that our loving cats had brought home for some live entertainment. Then Louie one of the Chinese Crested dogs got sick – vomiting and diarrhoea for three days. Finally, the tractor broke down, this was followed by my one-hour car service going into a seven-hour repair job. The whole week just turned into an array of little storms being hurled at me. By the time I got to Sunday I was exhausted – both mentally and physically.

It's very easy to hand over the controls of your life verbally and wholeheartedly to God every morning – but don't do what I did. I handed it over and then I would take it back because I thought I could get the job done faster and better.

I do believe I was very convincing when I eventually gave my sermon – because I had lived through how not to do it. Yes, I did give God the controls first thing in the morning but then I would take them back shortly after.

We must learn to "Let go and let God". It's not easy to hand everything over but with constant prayer and help from the Holy Spirit it is possible to walk in supernatural peace knowing that God has us in the palm of His hand.

Prayer

Lord, I want to live a peaceful, joyful life, in spite of the stress life can throw at us – I know this can only happen if I release the controls of my life over to you daily. From today onwards I am going to stand firm on my commitment to surrendering every detail of my day to you, and no matter how turbulent or dark my day may get I will have the ability not to take back my concerns or worries. I thank you, Lord, that you have my back in everything that happens today and that your love for me is so strong that nothing can come between us. Amen

Purpose

Run your own race

Read Hebrews 12:1-12

"And let us run with perseverance the race marked out for us, fixing our eyes on Jesus, the author and perfecter of faith."

Hebrews 12:1b–2a

I was frustrated and annoyed – I wanted to be out there preaching, speaking and more active in my ministry for God. Many of my friends were doing what I wanted to do while I just watched on. I felt like God had just parked me up on the side of the road. I prayed for clarity and wisdom as I battled with my frustrations. My prayer was answered with a dream.

I dreamt that I was in a race, a running race, and that every other competitor was overtaking me. I was becoming more and more stressed as people flew past me, while my legs were getting heavier and heavier. I could see the finish line but was frustrated because I was behind everybody. When I crossed the line, in what seemed like last place, a little man came running up to me jumping up and down with such joy shouting, "You won! You won!" and proceeded to hang a medal around my neck. I tried to explain to him that he must have been looking at the wrong race because I had come in last. But he kept saying, "You won! You won!" Then suddenly I woke up.

This dream felt so real – actually so real my whole body felt like I'd run a race. But what did it mean? As I sat and processed this dream over breakfast it dawned on me that God was showing me that we are all in a race and if we keep our eyes just focused on Him then yes, we will win. It doesn't matter what others are doing, we must not compare ourselves to them, we are all on different paths. If we focus on other humans, it detracts from what God has planned for us; sometimes God puts us in a lay-by while He shapes and moulds us for the next part of the journey.

By depending solely on God, a path will open up that is uniquely for us; if we go our own way our giftings cannot be utilised. We must run our own race, not the race of someone else. He has already planned our race, and the only way to stay on track is by not letting go of God's hands.

Prayer

Lord my God, I thank you for the many blessings you give me; the breath of life, the gift of salvation and a race which is mine alone. Teach me, Lord, not to focus on what others are doing but to keep my eyes solely on you. I know that I am fearfully and wonderfully made and that the race ahead will have its ups and downs, but if I can stay connected to you through prayer and obedience, I will win my race and spend the rest of my days in eternity with you, my Father and my King. Amen

Forfeiting your soul

Read Mark 8:34-38

"What good is it for someone to gain the whole world, yet forfeit their soul?"

Mark 8:36

In my earlier years/twenties and thirties I lived to compete not only in sports but in everything. Life was all about winning trophies, accolades and awards; there was nothing else. My drive, passion and disciplined lifestyle allowed me to push myself every day to new limits – but at what cost?

No sooner had I finished one competition I would be preparing for the next; it was like a never-ending merry-go-round. And when I did stop, which only happened when I was injured and laid up in hospital, I had this uneasy feeling that life didn't really make sense. As the years went by and the merry-go-round carried on at full speed, I began to realise that winning and achieving everything I had ever wanted did not fulfil my dream of finding meaning and purpose. I was always expecting to feel so much more fulfilled after winning a race but instead I felt the opposite. I felt empty on the inside and I didn't know why.

It was only when everything I treasured was removed from my life that I came face to face with the truth; sometimes in life we are given opportunities to reassess where we are going. For me the turning point in my life came when for the first time in my sporting career I had failed to qualify as one of six riders for the Irish Team. This totally threw me into an emotional downward spiral – it was like my personality had been stripped away and my purpose for living removed. It was in this time that Jesus stepped in and took me by the hand and opened my eyes to the truth – showing me that surrendering everything over to Him gave me everything I'd ever wanted. "For whoever wants to save their life will lose it, but whoever loses their life for me will find it" (Matthew 16:25).

Opportunities to see the right answers and find the right way in life don't always come in the shape of celebrations and happy events, but normally appear when things don't go as planned. Or should I say don't go your way! I could have stayed on the merry-go-round and obtained more and more trophies, yet I knew there could be so much more.

When darkness and an emptiness overtake don't give up; call out to God and see how He answers – you may be surprised! Light does come out of the darkness. Jesus came to bring light into the world and it's through Him we can step into a life full of hope, peace and freedom.

Prayer

Lord, show me that even in the dark and gloomy times, you can turn my life around in a blink of an eye. Help me to understand that sometimes these trials are sent for a reason. Allow me to let go of the things in my life that stop me experiencing more of you; allow me to let go of burdens, habits and wrong motives that chain me to this world. I want to walk in the supernatural, I want to walk with you, Lord, and I know this is only possible once I let go of worldly possessions and desires and put you first in my life. I thank you, my King, my God, that as of today, I will have eyes only for you. Amen

Let the doors slam shut!

Read Luke 10:38-42

> *"But few things are needed – or indeed only one. Mary has chosen what is better, and it will not be taken away from her."*
>
> **Luke 10:42**

I was frustrated as nothing much was happening in my life, so I began the search for a new project. I found a few possible projects but nothing that had me jumping with enthusiasm. In my quiet time whilst I prayed into my frustrations God kept giving me this image. I was sitting in a round room with many doors – each door signified an opportunity, another adventure and a new project. But as I sat in the middle of this room, each of the doors started slamming shut – one after the other. I sat there in a sealed room just me on a chair. God was shutting down all possible projects and new ventures. But "Why?"

The answer I got was "stop and listen." The vision was simple and clear: it was time to rest and sit at His feet in silence. This was not what I had planned. Like many, I love being busy as it makes me feel like I've achieved something. But God sees things very different – so when He shuts down all your busyness then it's an opportunity to take time out to sit and be with Him. Just Him without any distractions. Time in the presence of God allows us to get a better perspective of where we should be going but, above all, it re-routes us back to the source of everything – God. Jesus shows us in the story of Martha and Mary that being busy must come second to our time with Him.

So many times in my life God has stopped me dead in my tracks and said in a compassionate voice "enough". We all need to press that reset button sometimes to realign ourselves – most of us don't – so that's when God steps in as a loving father and does it for us. Say thank you and take the time to enjoy no distractions, no deadlines, no busyness. In that time, saturate yourself in His presence and ask God to open your spiritual ears and eyes so that your relationship with Him will deepen. There is nothing on this planet that comes close to the restoration and transformation that happens within each of us when we spend time alone with God.

Remember we each have a choice. Even if God closes all the doors to get our attention, we still have the freedom to choose. Some will knock down or even bulldoze through these closed doors out of total frustration – instead we need to consider why are we doing this and what the outcome of this will be? Jesus wants to connect and show us things, sometimes this happens only when we stop and sit at His feet and listen.

Prayer

My God, my King, there is nothing on this earth that can compare with sitting at your feet. In your presence I feel strong and complete, in your presence I feel I'm at home. Open my spiritual heart, ears and eyes so that I can clearly see, feel and hear you. Amen

Signposts

Read Psalm 32:1-11

> *"I will instruct you and teach you in the way you should go; I will counsel you with my loving eye on you."*
>
> **Psalm 32:8**

In my quiet time I kept seeing images of a very calm lake, and alongside this image the word *peace*. I kept a record of the times I kept seeing the same picture but had no clue what it meant. A couple of weeks went by and then the image changed. Now the lake stayed calm, but a huge black wave loomed on the horizon; a storm was going to hit. I mentioned this in our prayer group but still had no idea what it meant – if it meant anything at all – could it be just my imagination playing tricks?

During this time I was trying to prepare a sermon for the following Sunday but just couldn't come up with the right message – every time this happened, I knew I wouldn't be preaching.

"Iona, can we swap Sundays? I will preach this coming weekend if you do mine in two weeks," asked the minister Lyndon. "And let me know if you want to do the scheduled gospel reading Mark 4:35-41."

I jumped at the chance of changing but was reluctant to do the scheduled reading, I normally did my own theme but felt drawn to checking out the Bible passage. As I read the passage I nearly fell off my chair backwards; it was Jesus calming the storm. As I read the story, the images I'd seen flashed in front of me, "That day when evening came, he said to his disciples, 'Let us go over to the other side.' Leaving the crowd behind, they took him along, just as he was, in the boat. There were also other boats with him. A furious squall came up, and the waves broke over the boat, so that it was nearly swamped. Jesus was in the stern, sleeping on a cushion. The disciples woke him and said to him. 'Teacher, don't you care if we drown?' He got up rebuked the wind and said to the waves, 'Quiet! Be still!' Then the wind died down and it was completely calm. He said to his disciples, 'Why are you so afraid? Do you still have no faith?' They were terrified and asked each other, 'Who is this? Even the wind and the waves obey him!'"

I knew this topic was important and I diligently and prayerfully studied the passage. The words came naturally, and the message flowed – not from me but the Holy Spirit. It was a message that at that time needed to be heard. I love the way God guides us and shows us His thoughts through the images and pictures that He gives. That preaching was so relevant to me and those who heard it. By keeping a journal and recording thoughts, images and dreams we allow God to guide us – even if they don't make sense at the time – just wait and if they are from God, confirmation and clarity on their meaning will come at the right time.

Prayer

Lord, teach me to expect the unexpected in my daily life. Give me a discerning mind to know when new ideas, visions, images and thoughts are from you. I know that this attitude of watching and being conscious of everything opens my spiritual ears and eyes to what you want to say. Enlighten me, guide me and use me I pray. Amen

Don't be a hamster

Read Matthew 6:25-34

"But seek first his kingdom and his righteousness, and all these things will be given to you as well."
Matthew 6:33

At the end of each day, I love ticking my "To do" projects off my list, I get a real sense of achievement from this. So throughout the day I feel the need to be on the move all the time which allows me to complete my tasks. As the years have flown by, however, I've realised that this is not beneficial in any way, shape or form, and, as my faith and knowledge have increased, I no longer want to do my own things; instead I want to do what God has planned for me.

One of the Bible verses that has guided me towards a purposeful life is Psalm 127:1:

"Unless the LORD builds the house, the builders labour in vain. Unless the LORD watches over the city, the guards stand watch in vain."

To undertake projects, jobs and hobbies outside of God's will leaves you feeling like a dog chasing its tail. Going around in circles is rather pointless. I have a habit of picking up a project and running with it and then it all goes pear shaped when I hit a brick wall. "God, what happened there?" I would shout. I know why it happened; I never prayed about it, I just decided this was what I wanted to do. My husband Jeff says I'm like a hamster on a wheel when I start on a new project – I just don't stop. Over the years Jesus has stepped in on numerous occasions and stopped me from following certain career paths. I've learnt when He says no there is a very good reason. It's when I've looked back years later, I understand why God jumped in and redirected my steps.

We all want to know what God's will is for our lives – none of us want to labour in vain. By seeking Him first – by actively listening and praying, God can reposition you back on the right track. If He's your focus throughout the day and you are obedient to His commandments the road before you will be made straight. And if you are struggling to hear His voice in a situation, pray that God will close or open the door depending on His will for your life. But above all seek Jesus first and watch as He repositions you and aligns you back to His will.

Prayer

Lord, I pray right now that you remove or stop all the unwanted activities in my daily life that interfere with the plan you have in place for me. Please don't allow me to waste the time you've given me doing meaningless pastimes when I could be doing kingdom work. Give me a seeker's heart to seek you first in everything. Guide me throughout the day, closing those doors that should be closed and opening doors that lead to kingdom activities. Amen

Worship

Let go and connect!

Read John 4:1-26

"God is spirit, and his worshippers must worship in the Spirit and in truth."

John 4:24

I love spending the weekends at the farm when it's just me and the animals. After feeding the dogs, cats, horses and taking the dogs for a forty-five-minute hike it's time for worship.

Many years ago, I would have never dreamt of dancing, singing, and raising my hands in my daily time with God – now I cannot live without it. Having been brought up a Catholic and then worshipping in many different denominations I've realised that worship must come from the heart. It does not come from man-made traditions or rituals – worship comes from a passion – a passionate heart that knows the truth about who Jesus is. In my early years in a Catholic convent, I would do almost anything to get out of a church service. I found that the most effective one was pretending to faint, this always worked a treat! Back then I didn't really know Jesus so how could I worship something I didn't know? The more I've learnt about Jesus the more I have wanted to worship Him. Worshipping our Lord comes naturally when we are in a personal relationship with Him. I look back and smile when I remember the first time I experienced a church where they raised their hands and sang; I froze on the spot with shock. But as I got to know Jesus on a deeper level, I found it impossible not to be overly passionate in worship and lift my hands to the heavens.

I have experienced many breakthroughs and revelations in my worship time – why? Because I connect directly to the source – the source of everything – Jesus. To get totally lost in praising and glorifying God allows the Holy Spirit to overflow in you and guide you. I'm not sure what my neighbours think of my weekend worship sessions; I would say by now they are used to the worship music echoing across the valley from our farm and thankfully they can't see me prancing around on the veranda!

Having no distractions and not worrying about what people think must be utmost in your worship time, whether in church or outside, God knows your heart. I know I've missed out on quality time with God at many worship services as I've been preoccupied with my own thoughts and the people around me. When we focus on God alone, we release ourselves into His heavenly presence.

Let go and connect with Jesus, humbly come into His presence, prepare your hearts and let the Holy Spirit guide you.

Prayer

Lord, I want to focus on you alone, help me to break the chains of distraction right now. My goal is to worship in the Spirit so that no earthly thoughts can enter. There is nothing that compares to being in your presence, there is nothing that can pull me away from the source of everything. Without you I can do nothing – teach me, Lord, how to worship with a pure heart so that my faith will deepen and my knowledge of you would grow. Amen

Beware of idols

Read Matthew 22:34-40

"Jesus replied: 'Love the Lord your God with all your heart and with all your soul and with all your mind.'"
Matthew 22:37

We were born to worship, unfortunately we can worship the wrong thing without even realising we are doing it. For years I was happy bobbing along with Jesus, feeling content and happy, but there was a nagging feeling deep within me that said there was so much more; I prayed for clarity but was unaware where this would lead me.

During this time, I was fully involved with my long-distance endurance racing. I was coming up to eight years on the Irish equestrian team and loving every minute. In between all the horse training and competitions, I studied the Bible an hour a day, prayed, took weekly communion, and had awesome Christian fellowship with the couple who had led me to Jesus. I thought I had the perfect life – I had Jesus and I had my sport – what else could I ask for?

Having always qualified for the big international races as one of six riders to represent Ireland I was mortified when my horse became ill prior to one of the qualifying races; this meant I lost my place for the up-and-coming World Equestrian Games in the USA. I felt like God had abandoned me, especially as He knew what this meant to me. I was angry and hurt to the point I felt like someone had died in the family. My whole world as I knew it fell apart. My identity and who I was had always been linked with my sports and my competitions. Having that removed left me feeling empty, vulnerable and helpless. It was during this time that God showed me where my priorities lay; it was my obsession with racing and my horses that took the number-one slot in my life. Once I realised this, I knew in my heart that God had never abandoned me; I had abandoned Him. Even though Jesus was part of my life He wasn't the most important part. It was in this awakening moment I decided to submit everything over to Jesus, which included my racing. That day of surrender turned my life upside down in the most amazing way. And in that letting go, I felt all my burdens disappear and I encountered a freedom and peace that I'd never felt before.

We were born to worship our Creator and Father in heaven – it's in this pure focused worship that we transform ourselves into who God created us to be and this sets us on our unique path towards eternal life.

Prayer

Almighty God, show me if there is anything in my life right now that is interfering with my relationship with you. Open my spiritual eyes to the possibility that there may be an obstacle that needs to be removed or repositioned. I want to live the life that you have planned for me – I know this can only happen if I surrender everything over to you. Lord, I give you control of my life; every second and every minute of my day I surrender over to you right now. Amen

Please stop the spinning!

Read Psalm 138:1-8

"May they sing of the ways of the LORD, for the glory of the LORD is great."

Psalm 138:5

Teaching your large fifty-kilo dog to dance, as in spinning around and jumping up when you clap for a double high five, is awesome but sometimes it can all backfire.

I was in the process of mucking out a stable whilst Shiraz lay comfortable, sleeping on the straw. I asked her to move, she ignored me so I placed the pitch fork down and clapped my hands to wake her up. Bad move . . . the next thing I knew I was on my back, lying on the concrete floor. Shiraz had obeyed what I'd taught her. My head hurt from hitting the concrete, but I was still breathing so I accepted it was my fault and carried on.

Ten days later I awoke feeling nauseous, the whole room was spinning – and no, I hadn't been drinking! I was diagnosed with benign positional vertigo, which in layman's terms is an inner ear malfunction from crystals being dislodged from a fall or head trauma. For the next seven years I had to take medication and I was unable to ever lay down flat. If I did, I would have yet another spinning seasick episode which could last for days. With no known cure I just had to live with it.

I did live with it until one day all that changed. Kate, a close friend of mine, and I attended a three-day Christian worship conference in Melbourne. The conference was beyond awesome – it was like I'd been transported to heaven and back. Worshipping Jesus in a stadium with 30,000 other Christians was mind blowing. At the end of the conference USA pastor Bill

Johnson asked if anyone had an inner right ear issue to please stand – I jumped to my feet along with several others and we were prayed for. I never thought much about my ear until a week later I realised I had been totally healed. Just like that! Now I could go back to the gym, I could roll over in bed and not worry about an onset of another spinning session and I could go to the dentist without taking lots of tablets beforehand.

When we gather to worship healing takes place. Over those three days I know many people at the conference were healed – many of whom were not physically prayed for. It's in the worshipping, either collectively or individually, that Jesus moves to show His love and grace; heaven moves to earth both physically and spiritually.

Prayer

Lord, I thank you that I can worship you in everything I do today. I can sing quietly or loudly of your wonderous deeds; you hear me and I feel your healing both spiritually and physically when I open my heart unconditionally. It's like the heavens open and your glory descends. How awesome is it that you love me and care for me. How amazing is it that you want to connect with me – Lord, I just want more of you. Amen

Turn the mundane into joy

Read Colossians 3:1-25

> *"Whatever you do, work at it with all your heart, as working for the Lord, not for human masters."*
>
> **Colossians 3:23**

I have been blessed to have a bit of a jet-set life, so when lockdown came because of COVID-19 this stopped my travel dead in its tracks. Now I was on the farm in Australia surrounded by cows, horses, dogs and cats plus the scary and unusual Australian wildlife. Months rolled into a year and the daily routine was beginning to be a little monotonous. My fast-paced life of skipping around the world seemed almost like a dream.

My whole perspective on farm life changed when I realised that this was where God wanted me, and He was watching to see what I would do with the environment I'd been placed in. To help me become aware of the importance of walking with Jesus throughout the day I memorised these two Bible verses.

'"Whatever you do, do it all for the glory of God" (1 Corinthians 10:31) and "Whatever you do, work at it with all your heart" (Colossians 3:23).

When I felt the blanket of boredom descend on my daily routine, I would recite these words and it changed my whole perspective. From mixing the horse feeds to washing buckets, cleaning the dog run, poo-picking, to my least favourite activity ironing – God's words instilled in me vigour, passion, and joy in these daily chores. As my thought process changed it also dawned on me that when we do our work with passion and do it for the glory of God, we are showing our Father and Creator that we are devoted to Him, that we love and revere Him. Worship can come in many forms, including what we consider to be as mundane and boring. We can worship God through our daily activities when we do each chore with all our heart and soul – and do it to glorify God. Do this and watch your dull routine turn into a joyous activity that elevates you closer to Jesus.

Prayer

Lord, walking with you each day gives me a joy and peace that is indescribable – the mundane jobs are no longer mundane because now I do everything, even those things that I may consider boring, to give you glory. I will worship you and give you glory in all my activities from when I awake until I lay my head to rest. May your glory shine through my daily duties so that your light shines out into the community and further. Amen

The power of worship

Read Psalm 150:1-6

"Let everything that has breath praise the LORD. Praise the LORD."

Psalm 150:6

True heartfelt worship brings a new dimension to our lives. When we worship from our very hearts the doors of heaven open wider and a connection is established that allows the divine to be experienced on earth.

When we first started our Prayer, Praise and Pecan (we meet under the pecan tree) gathering on the farm we started to notice unusual things. The first was that as we sang hundreds of birds would circle above us – it was like they were joining in with the worship. On other occasions we would see birds that we'd never seen before. When we brought dogs to the worship, they would all stop barking and just sleep – my Beauceron Shiraz is a Prayer, Praise and Pecan fanatic – she takes centre stage – lying on her back just soaking up the atmosphere. Our farm animals also participate, all our horses come down from their paddocks and stand along the surrounding fence lines, transfixed as we sing and dance.

To stand outside with arms raised to the heavens and to sing aloud with God's creation is the most amazing experience. Every time we gather under the tree, we see God's creation join in with our praise. On one occasion, after two hours of singing and prayer we were amazed to see green buds appear all over the pecan tree. Prior to this our massive tree looked almost dead – worship brings things alive, and it brings healing, it allows us to encounter Jesus in a very tangible way. His presence and His glory always seem to be present under the pecan tree. Recently we had a contractor come to the farm who messaged me after he left saying, "This might sound strange, but I felt the presence of God on your property" – he had been working by the pecan tree. I told him about PPP and he is planning to join us with his family.

Worshipping our King, our Lord, the great I AM, opens the gates of heaven and connects us with God's love, peace and healing. It brings a divine flow of the supernatural – invisible power that becomes visible in worship.

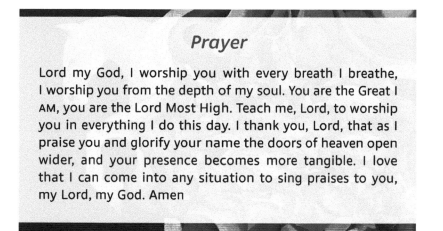

Prayer

Lord my God, I worship you with every breath I breathe, I worship you from the depth of my soul. You are the Great I AM, you are the Lord Most High. Teach me, Lord, to worship you in everything I do this day. I thank you, Lord, that as I praise you and glorify your name the doors of heaven open wider, and your presence becomes more tangible. I love that I can come into any situation to sing praises to you, my Lord, my God. Amen

Strength

Whatever it takes

Read Ephesians 2:1-10

"For we are God's handiwork, created in Christ Jesus to do good works, which God prepared in advance for us to do."

Ephesians 2:10

There are times in life when you come to what looks like a crossroad. The path ahead is unknown and turning either right or left seems to have even less appeal. What do you do?

Not long ago on one of my trips back to Dubai – I had come to the point where I had finished all my projects and had probably, for the very first time in my life, no commitments. After about three weeks of relaxing I began to get itchy feet. I had been spending much of my time in prayerful meditation and was loving my time just sitting at the feet of Jesus. But I knew my season of relaxation was coming to an end; this was exciting but daunting; what should I do in a situation like this? Just sit and wait for God to make a move? Nothing seemed to be happening, so I prayed and prayed.

It was only when I got on my knees and prayed, "Whatever it takes, Lord – I'll do whatever you want me to do!" did He step in and open a door. Be very careful when you pray like this as God will take you up on it. I knew in my heart that this would trigger a response, but I wasn't expecting the next move. Totally out of the blue I was approached to help coordinate a new high-profile anti-slavery initiative run by the Vatican, Church of England and a Muslim philanthropist. This was not what I had in mind, so prayed that the doors would close but they kept opening and I knew God was saying, "I want you to do this." I spent a great deal of time trying to talk Him out of this decision but to no avail!

For the next eighteen months I travelled between Dubai, London, Rome and New York organising high-profile events at the United Nations, Lambeth Palace and the Vatican. It was a role that had many ups and downs, but it was one that helped me grow in strength and personality. I wouldn't have put myself in this job, not in a million years, yet God has given each of us unique gifts and talents that He wants to use and He will provide the opportunities for us – so don't be afraid to pray "Whatever it takes, Lord – I will do whatever you want!" And wait for the adventure to begin . . .

Prayer

Lord, there is nothing more important in my life than to do your will. It's so easy to step off in the wrong direction without knowing it; reposition me, Lord, back on the path you have designated for me. Lord, I will do whatever it takes – use me for your kingdom purposes. Amen

No limits

Read Ephesians 3:14-21

"Now to him who is able to do immeasurably more than all we ask or imagine, according to his power that is at work within us."

Ephesians 3:20

I love singing and worshipping – so when the thought of learning the guitar suddenly popped into my head I jumped at the chance. I bought myself a guitar and I learnt all the basics from a lovely young man on YouTube. OK it's a slow process but I do thirty minutes every day. Some days it's good, other days I tell God He should put His earmuffs on! I know I'm not musically gifted, but I know with practice and with divine intervention I will get to a level where I can worship without causing earache to my companions.

My friends weren't convinced however. "Do you read music?" asked my friend. "Nope and I've never really played an instrument except the recorder in school and then I could only play 'Three Blind Mice'." We laughed. "Then you have no chance!" I ignored the negative remark because I've learnt over the years that listening to humans on what I can and cannot do has no bearing on God's will for my life. When God puts a desire in your heart don't let the devil creep in and tell you that you're not good enough, you're not strong enough – you're just not enough!

Many years prior, on my road to becoming a journalist I had learnt not to lose hope when obstacles appeared. From the beginning the road was bumpy – I had failed English at school and had also received the lowest grade in my class. Yet after my skiing accident I had this urge to write. I remember writing a story about the death of Formula One driver Ayrton Senna... I was there that fatal day. I asked a friend to comment on my writing and he did: "Stick to sports – that's beyond bad." Those words stuck with me; that day I gave up on my dream of becoming a writer – until God intervened years later and showed me otherwise. I went on to become an equine photographic journalist for international publications and I published my first book. Don't let others set your limits for you or take your dreams away from you.

Don't limit yourself – be strong in the Lord and pray into ideas that pop into your mind – don't discard them no matter how crazy they might seem to you or your friends. God will close the door if it's not for you. He will make the path straight and guide you if it's His will.

Prayer

Lord, one of your many promises is that you will guide me in the right direction if I submit my plans to you. Teach me, Lord, to submit everything to you daily and allow me to move when you give me a new idea or plan for my life. Give me the wisdom to follow through on those thoughts that may seem stupid, crazy, or just so out of my reach. Give me the understanding that as a child of the living God there are no limits. Amen

Be thankful

Read Philippians 4:4-9

"Do not be anxious about anything, but in every situation, by prayer and petition, with thanksgiving, present your requests to God. And the peace of God which transcends all understanding, will guard your hearts and your minds in Christ Jesus."
Philippians 4:6-7

It was one disaster after the other, the situation was so bad and I was struggling to pray because I couldn't stop thinking about all the problems we had on the farm. I kept playing all these different scenarios over in my head which kept fuelling all the negative sides to the problem; it was like a full-on battle in my head, and I had no control.

I couldn't get my head above the water, I was drowning, and I couldn't see a way to stop it. But there was – it's very unnatural to say thank you when you feel like your world is falling apart – but my Bible reading on this particular day was "be thankful in every situation". And yes, I had read this and knew this verse but! My human thoughts just laughed at this command, "How on earth is this going to help me sort this mess out?"

I ignored my feelings and every time a negative thought popped into my head, I said thank you to God for the situation I was in. I would pray, "Lord, I thank you for this challenge. I don't understand why this is happening, but I know you're in control so thank you." The more I said "thank you" the more I became clear headed and felt a peace settle over me – one that I could not explain.

By saying "thank you' it triggered a divine response from heaven. My mind started to clear, and the negative thoughts slowed down to the point where it was difficult for them to have a hold of me. So, when the Bible says "The peace of God, which transcends all understanding, will guard your hearts and your minds in Christ Jesus" (Philippians 4:7) it does – it's a supernatural remedy that allows us to overcome the devil's mind games.

Next time you're in a situation that overwhelms you – don't wait for your emotions to take control or overwhelm you; say "thank you" to God for taking control and hand it all to Him, and watch His peace surround you.

Prayer

Lord, remind me to be thankful always even when it doesn't feel natural. How amazing is it that you can transform my life with the words I speak and think. Lord, open my spiritual eyes and ears so that I get a better understanding of what it means to be thankful even when I'm scared, lonely and confused. I want to walk through this life with a thankful heart so your joy and peace will surround me. Amen

Bless your enemies

Read 6:27-36

"Bless those who curse you, pray for those who ill-treat you."

Luke 6:28

Life would be so much better if we got on well with everyone but that is definitely not the case on planet earth. Heaven, yes; it will be the perfect place, no judging, no gossiping, no racism – just joy, laughter and peace as we work and play under the loving eyes of our Father. So how do we cope when we come face to face with hatred and abuse? Jesus clearly tells us we must love our enemies; it's not always easy but it's possible with His help.

I learnt a very big lesson when I got verbally attacked by someone who I thought was a friend – this was a person I was in contact with daily and even though I knew of their reputation I battled on thinking I could change them. I was wrong. On this occasion I had to let go as it was turning into a very toxic relationship; there are some situations when God will step in and say enough is enough. When I made the decision to walk away from this friendship, I felt a massive burden suddenly lift off my shoulders and calm descended. When this happened, I realised that I had done the right thing. The emotional turmoil I'd felt disappeared leaving me with a clear mind and a peace I couldn't explain.

Now I had many questions – how, by walking away from a so-called friend or enemy, was I loving them? And secondly, how could I repair the invisible scars on my heart and that dull heartache of losing a friend? I realised that as I prayed for them and prayed blessings on them daily that I was also healing, and I knew that every prayer I prayed for my friend was heard and that Jesus was in control of their situation. Maybe one day in the future we may reconnect, but for now, through heart-felt prayers and daily blessings, I knew Jesus was ministering to them. Loving your enemies doesn't always mean you need to constantly be in communication with them, but we do need to be available if they cry out for help. And if that does happen you must then allow the Holy Spirit to guide you. Praying for your enemies daily can turn their lives around and yours.

Prayer

Lord, I know that there will be times when people will irritate me and there will be times when I will lose my temper – Lord, I pray that in these situations I will stop, wait, and say a silent prayer. Help me to see each human as you do; a child of the living God. Create in me a heart that is so full of love that even when I am threatened and hurt by another that I do not react in malice, but I act only in love. I pray that through my loving actions they will see you and come to know you. Amen

More sales please!

Read Philippians 2:12-18

"For it is God who works in you to will and to act in order to fulfil his good purpose."
Philippians 2:13

When I finished my biography *Racing on Empty* I stormed into action with an elaborate public relations and social media campaign. Yes, I sort of prayed into this but looking back I can say that I was doing it regardless of what God wanted. After spending three years writing this book, I felt confident in myself that this was the way to go. I truly believed God would approve so I never really handed over the promotional part to Him. Plus, as all the proceeds were going to a charity and the book was about my walk with Jesus then I would have His blessing.

Over a six-month period, I invested a great deal of money into the advertising and marketing – I had a new flashy website and had received great media coverage, but the book sales moved slowly. Even with five-star reviews and great write-ups I battled to understand why the book wasn't selling by the hundreds – why had it not become a best-seller? OK, we were in the middle of a pandemic but that may have given some people plenty of time to read, but life doesn't always work out that way. The book sales were slow – people just weren't buying.

A year on and I look back a great deal wiser – I had done all this in my own strength whilst God looked on waiting for me to slow down. When I did stop and ask why – I felt Him say it's all about timing and He gave me these words: "For it is God who works in you to will and to act in order to fulfil his good purpose." I knew if I had carried on with my plans, I would derail the purposes that He had planned for me. My aspirations for the book and how I perceive success are very different from God's. I realised even if one reader had come to know Jesus through my book then that was enough. That one person could go on to spread the gospel message in a community that needed to hear the good news of Jesus.

The lesson here is to let God into every area of your life – move and work in His strength and only His. He is then able to lead you; if you've already started without Him, stop and go back to the beginning – He'll reset your path and guide you so that you fulfil His good purposes. Don't presume you know better than God!

Prayer

Lord, I thank you for leading me in all areas of my life. I pray today that if I've run ahead of myself in some areas, take me back to the beginning and let me start again – this time in prayer with listening ears. I thank you, Lord, that you are a God of restoration and a God of second chances. I am sorry for those times in my life when I have bulldozed through the day and forgotten about you. I know, Lord, that all my plans, hobbies and ideas come to nothing if they are not built on your will for my life. From today onwards I will not initiate anything without talking to you first. Amen

God
Answered

God answered

Read 1 Kings 18:41-46

"'Go and look toward the sea,' he told his servant. And he went up and looked. 'There is nothing there,' he said. Seven times Elijah said, 'Go back.'"
1 Kings 18:43

I collapsed exhausted onto my bed, I had no more tears – I could cry no longer. My eyes were swollen and my head hurt; after days of continual praying I could pray no more, I couldn't think and I didn't want to think. I felt numb.

I hadn't slept for three nights and I was exhausted. I sat perched on the edge of my bed; how nice would it be to roll over, go to sleep and then wake up to find this was all just one horrid dream . . .

Three days ago, we were overjoyed when our Arabian mare Zara gave birth to her first foal – a little filly. We had prayed for a girl and that's exactly what we got, but within a couple of hours we knew things weren't right. She was struggling to stand and was making some very strange motions with her neck, as if she was in pain. She kept walking into the stable wall and seemed unable to focus on objects – it was like she had been deprived of oxygen. Instead of wanting to find her mum's milk she would stand staring at the stable wall; when she did drink, which was rare, she would only gulp a few mouthfuls and then collapse on the ground. Every hour we would help her to stand so that she could get the all-important sustenance for those first few days.

We called the vet and as we waited for him to arrive I texted everybody I knew and asked for prayer. I knew God was watching and hearing our cries for help. The vet was concerned but told us to stay positive, explaining that she should improve. He had also suggested that it was best to monitor her throughout the night, just in case she deteriorated. That night I got up every two hours to help our little filly stand and feed. It was heartbreaking to see her struggling so much, but I knew God could turn this nightmare around at any time.

Morning came but unfortunately the news was not good; she now had colic so we rushed to town to get some medication from the vet. After treating her, I laid hands on her and prayed again. Immediately a big burst of wind erupted from under her tail; she had a build-up of gas inside her which could have been lethal. We were overjoyed that the colic had subsided, but our joy was short lived as she soon started to show signs of sepsis, a dangerous inflammation in the joints.

That evening, myself and Melinda, who works for us, and two vets gathered in the stable to discuss the way forward for our little filly. She was not even two days old and had so many ailments; it was heart-wrenching to see her rolling around in such pain. The vets decided she needed to go to an equine emergency hospital as there was nothing they could do for her. The nearest hospital was three hours away, though, and in another state which was in lockdown. After many calls we found that no one was able to help us transport mum and baby – we would have to pray that our foal survived the night in the hope that we could get transport the following day.

I walked back to the house and sat down at our kitchen table. There was nothing else I could do for the foal. I felt my heart breaking and I cried and cried. I pleaded with God for a miracle. I was overwhelmed with sorrow and confused – why was God letting this happen?

I sat on the bed, drained, exhausted and unable to pray. I couldn't face going back to the stables, I had nothing left in me. Then I felt God direct me to a book that was hidden at the bottom of my bedside table. I hadn't touched this book in over a year; it was a 360-day devotional written by Charles Spurgeon. I opened it and read the evening devotional for that day, the twenty-eighth of September. The scripture heading was, "*Go again seven times*" followed by the words, "*Success is certain when the Lord has promised it. Although you may have pleaded it is not possible that the Lord should be deaf when His people are earnest in a matter which concerns His glory . . . So far from being crushed by repeated disappointment, faith is animated to plead more fervently with her God . . . Plead the precious blood with unceasing importunity and it shall be with you according to your desire.*" As I read these words it was like God was speaking to me in a very clear concise voice, "Go back to the stables and pray again. And keep going back."

I leapt up and headed back to the stables; in my heart I felt that she had already been healed, I just knew it. As I walked into the stable, I stood in awe as I saw an orange glow in and around the mare and foal; I knew that something had changed. I crouched down quietly and lightly touched the foal on her bottom. She stood up immediately without any help from me. I couldn't believe my eyes. This was the first time she had managed to stand on her own without help. Our filly seemed a great deal brighter and livelier and at one point she started trotting in circles. I couldn't comprehend what was happening; was I dreaming? Was I so tired that I was imagining this? After forty-five minutes of watching her and repeatedly thanking God for what was happening, she lay down to sleep and I returned to the house and set my alarm so I could check on mum and baby at one-thirty a.m.

On returning to the stables our little princess was up and walking around – she looked like a different foal. Her eyes were bright, she was nibbling and playing with the hay, and she was drinking. I knelt and continued praying; this was a miracle.

For the first time in three days, I went back to bed, took my work clothes off and put on my pyjamas. I knew God had answered our prayers. When my alarm went off at four a.m. I checked the stable camera on my phone and stared in wonder – she was standing and busy investigating her surroundings! I smiled and went back to sleep.

That morning we let her out into the paddock and watched in amazement as she cantered and played; she showed no sign of any illnesses. When the vet arrived, he was shocked; he had never seen a foal recover like this before. I couldn't stop thanking God for this miracle.

The story doesn't stop there however . . . we hadn't named her as it didn't seem right to do this previously, but now I prayed for a name, one which would glorify God. I googled names and more names, then all of a sudden one jumped out at me – Arabella. It sounded strong and bold just like her. I decided to do a google search on the meaning of Arabella; my eyes locked on the words in wonder when I read the meaning: "God answered" or "yield to prayer".

This whole experience taught me a huge lesson – never stop praying even when you can't pray any more. God hears every word you utter; when you get to a point where you are unable to continue – listen to the quiet still voice of God and let Him direct and comfort you.

Prayer

Lord, teach me to be a fervent prayer warrior who never gives in to doubt or human weakness. Give me a lion's attitude, bold, strong and courageous, so that I can live a prayerful life knowing that everything and anything is possible with you. Thank you for using this little horse, Arabella, to show us that perseverance pays off and that even when we come to a point of absolute despair there is still hope in you. Thank you, Jesus. Amen